Chapter One

"Introduction"

Have you ever felt so frustrated about finding love because it never seems to work out? Why we always end up dating someone who will break our hearts so quickly? Or why can't life just match us up with our soul mate instead of putting us through this constant heartbreak over and over again? Have you ever asked yourself was my fault? Am I not that attractive? Or do you ask yourself questions like how come others found love so easily and here I am watching from the side? Or why is every guy the same? Was there ever a time when you gave up on love, but your conscience is too stubborn to let you? Have you ever been told constantly from others to be patient and your lover will come when you least expect it? Have you ever wondered why the one you cared about stopped caring about you? Lastly, have you ever asked yourself what would have life been like if he stayed?

I have been on many dates, but only seven of them affected my life in ways that made me the proud man I am today. That is what this story will be. This story is about how seven different men who I dated changed me to become the man I am proud to be today. I decided to write this story after a long drive in the rain. I was playing love songs, and it helped me realize my reality. I have dated about seven guys in my life, and each one is so different, and all of them ended just the same. Each one took a piece of my heart and it all ended with me never able to have my first boyfriend. I've never had a relationship with a guy before, and till this day on December 9th, 2016, I am still alone. I am going to share you a story about the seven guys I've dated. I will talk all about the sparks I felt, the first kiss, the first touch, and even the first time someone ever said "I love you," I won't be mentioning any real names so that I can protect their identities. To this day, I have become wiser, and smarter. However, I wasn't always. I use to be the type that would fall in love so quickly that I became the hopeless romantic clingy type. So I am asking you to please understand that it all happened when I was very young. My name is Lorenzo, and by the end of this story, you will see the man that I am proud to have become from all this. It all started with a young man named John.

Chapter Two

"My First"

My story began on July 12th, 2012. I was just an 18 years old who had just graduated from high school when I met John. Now, remember I have never done anything with a guy, and this first guy is what opened my world to the gay community. Everything all started when I was on a dating website. I logged on one Sunday afternoon, and I get a message from this white guy with Brown hair. We exchanged a few messages until he asked me out on a date. I was very nervous because this would be the first time I have ever been with a guy. John lived about 60 miles away from me. However, he was willing to make the drive out here.

So on July 12th, 2012 was the day of my first actual date with a guy. We decided to meet on the bottom floor of the mall around the center. As I was waiting for him, I turn around, and I see a guy looking at me from a distance. It felt a bit creepy, and I didn't know it was him, so I texted him. Once he got the text, he laughed and walked up to me.

The moment I heard his voice I automatically noticed that he sounded a bit feminine. I was a little weirded out for a moment because I came from a family that hates GAY PEOPLE, but he was so cute, and I pushed aside everything my parents had put in my mind about the LGBT community. My parents made my world seem as if gay people were looked down upon and I was too scared to be a part of that. I was afraid of being looked down upon as well.

Sometime during the date, I remember when John reached to hold my hand as we were walking. It was the first time I ever held someone's hand. I remember this feeling of how it felt so right. I felt a thousand butterflies flying around my heart. I even remember having a little smile on my face. The kind of smile where you tell yourself, "I can't believe I finally feel what sparks are like." However, I was afraid of what society would think if they saw me, so a couple of times I would just let go of his hand even though it felt excellent. Just being next to him made me feel happy. It was a feeling that I never felt before. I never thought that one touch felt so good and it made me feel whole. To hold his hand was scary, but it was so worth it all.

After walking around half the day. We went to my place, and we were also home alone. We went to my bedroom, and it was the first time I ever cuddled. Having his arms wrapped around me is something I could never forget. I remembered thinking, "So this is what it feels like to be loved." I loved that feeling of someone holding me. I never thought love would feel like this. I finally was able to feel what my friends felt whenever I saw them holding their partner's hand. I remembered laying on his chest and how soft it felt. I wished time stood still as I felt his body behind me keeping me warm. I turned around and looked at him. After we exchanged looks, I finally had my first kiss. Before we kissed, I remembered thinking, "I am going to go to Hell for this". It didn't matter because, for the first time in my life, I finally felt I was at a place where I was supposed to be. However, he sorta ruined it when he looked at me and said, "You're not very good at this huh?" He pointed out that I wasn't a good kisser, but hey could you blame me? It was my first kiss ever. I felt embarrassed, so I just kept kissing him until I got better. He eventually said, "Okay, you're getting there."

As the whole day continued, I remembered how his breath smelled so bad. It was so bad that I didn't even want to kiss him anymore, but I was falling for him so much that it wasn't even that important. He would always call me a dork because of my awkward personality. By the end of the day, we snuck into his truck in the mall parking lot. He had a blanket for us to lay on in the back. After holding each other, I remember feeling like I was falling for him. When he touched me all over, it felt like I was in love. I guess when you're young, that's how it's supposed to feel. That feeling of being wanted, held, cared for, loved, needed, and more.

I remember feeling like I just wanted to be with him forever. I remembered thinking wow this is who might become my first boyfriend and my first love. That day was the first day I felt that someone was mine. As each kiss we shared was another moment I felt happy. This kind of happiness is something a lot of people wanted and that day was the first day I felt it. Before we separated, he looked at me and said, "You know, I can't promise you a relationship..." The first thought was, "Really? You were my first kiss, you stole my virginity, and you are just gonna pretend like none of that mattered?" I looked at him and said, "It's okay." However, it was not okay. I felt a bit disappointed that he would do all these things for my first time and then not want to continue. My first everything with a guy was a big waste.

Him not wanting to become my first boyfriend after opening up my heart to the world I was so new to made me depressed for a few weeks. As weeks went by, I couldn't stop thinking about him. He was on my mind every single night. I don't know why he didn't decide to pursue anything else with me. All I knew for sure was I finally knew

what a broken heart felt like. This was the beginning of a pattern that I

never wanted.

Chapter Three

"When I was Someone's First"

Eric Sanchez was someone special; in fact out of all the guys I have dated I probably thought about him the most after he ended it with me. It was March 2013 when we met, and I was already 19 years old. It all started when I went on this new dating site. As lonely as I was I remembered messaging every single guy I found attractive. A few messaged back, yet one stuck out the most. You know when you do online dating, sometimes we get short messages and begin to wonder if they are even interested, or maybe you get the kind of moments where they don't even reply back to a few messages, or they don't even reply at all.

However, Eric was a little different. Eric looked kind of cute in his pictures. He has dark black hair, and he had a Hispanic background. He looked a little skinny, but it was the typical twink. After getting tired of the men who didn't show any interest in me, I decided to just forget about even replying to anybody else and just forget even trying. Suddenly Eric sent me a message, and it said, "Hey I'm not always on here so if you want to continue this, send me a text and we can chat from there." I was so surprised, so I ended up calling him on his cell phone. That first hello was sparkling to me. His voice was deep, and he was also around my age range. He wasn't out to his parents, so he had to talk over the phone when they weren't around.

I remembered laying on my bed talking to him for a bit. Wow, his voice made me want to look at the sky. Eric told me that he had never had a boyfriend and had never been with or kissed a guy before. I said to myself, "I'm not going to do what John did to me. If this is gonna happen, I promise to make this guy feel happy and make his first time with a guy very special, and if he wants to be with me, I will hold his hand and not let him experience what I did".

Eric lived 40 minutes from where I lived. However, he decided to take the train to come down to see me. We met up at the train station in my city. I remembered driving in and seeing him sitting down waiting for me. Once I parked, and I got out of my car. We walked towards each other, and the first thing we did was give each other a hug. His body felt so soft, and he smelled so good. He was so nervous, just like how I was when I met John. The first things I kept thinking was, I am going to show this guy a good time. I was excited; I remembered how his face felt against mine. It was so warm and smooth that I couldn't stop hugging him.

When we were driving to the mall, he kept looking at me, and I could tell he was nervous. We held hands as we drove with both our conjoined hands on my lap. I loved how nervous he was because it was so adorable. I wanted him to feel great and happy.

Once we parked, I had him walk towards me, and I held him. We held each other for a few minutes, and I love the smell on his body. It was probably what made me so attracted to him. Our chemistry was pretty perfect actually. Now I wasn't a big fan of PDA as you all know. So while at the mall, we would sneak in someone where no one could see us, and we would hug each other for as long as we could. When our hands touched, I felt butterflies.

Later that day, I took him to where I lived, and we laid on my bed, where we cuddled for the first time. I loved giving him kisses on the cheek until we looked at each other and for the first time, it felt like a drum roll as our lips were slowly moving towards each other. The moment we kissed, we looked at each other, and I asked, "is it me or did you just feel that?"

"Yes I did," he smiled. That spark between us ignited, and it was the spark that ignited way bigger than my first kiss with John. I loved kissing him, and we cuddled for a long period. By the time it was time for him to go home, we both were covered with hickeys. It was so worth it because we made each other happy.

For the whole week, we would text every day. I would text him good morning, and he would text me later in the day to ask how my day was. Out of all the guys I've dated, he showed that he cared about me whenever he would send me a text. That's when I knew he did like me. He was so amazing that I told him about my fear of birds because I was attacked by ducks when I was a kid. The sweetest thing he did was that whenever we walked around, he would scare off the birds so that I wouldn't be freaked out. He said to me, "I just like seeing you smile. It makes me happy when you do. It also makes you look adorable and even cuter."

I remember that we went to a photo booth one time and we took a picture. In one of those pictures, we had kissed. Eric loved them so much that he wanted to keep the original. He and I seemed so perfect together that we both agreed that we would work it out so that we could become boyfriends in the long run. I was so happy; I slept every night knowing my heart was safe.

One night, later on, we were at my place, and the lights were out. Things were getting very sexual as it started to escalate. I told him, "Wait, I don't want to move too fast. I don't want things to change if we do this." He said to me, "I promise, nothing is going to change." I then said, "I think I'm falling for you, Eric."

Eric looked into my eyes, "Lorenzo, I've never had anyone make me feel so special." The moment felt so right that we ended up making love that night. We didn't have sex or anything; we just ended up with half our clothes off. This boy right here in front of me was one of the best kissers I have ever dated.

When he drove off after that night, I had a bad feeling within my stomach. When I felt that feeling, I knew something bad was going to happen. The next day, he didn't text me all day until the end of the day while I was at the beach with friends; I get a text that said, "We need to talk. I am sorry, but you were right, we probably shouldn't have done what we did last night because, for some strange reason, I feel a bit numb emotionally. When you said that you were falling for me, it freaked me out, and I realized that maybe I am not ready for a relationship." He did this over text, and I told him we should talk about this in person, but he refused. It felt like an unresolved issue that was in my heart for months.

To make matters worse, two months later I checked on his Social Media account, and I saw that he was in a relationship. To make matters even more worse, he was in a relationship with John, the first guy I ever dated. After hearing that news, I fell to the ground as my heart couldn't take it. It felt like the world was crumbling on top of me. I remembered breathing heavily as I couldn't take in the news. It was like they both found each other while I got left in the dumps. The boy who I promised to love is the one who ended up being with someone who denied me the love I always wanted. I admit it's a very weird situation. Yes, it was a little stupid of me to feel sad about it, but Eric was something special to me, and as time went on, I moved on.

I ended up dating other guys, but they were nothing like Eric. So in March 2015, two years after he broke it off with me, I contacted him, and we agreed to meet up and reconnect. I was a bit thrilled because this time I would be the one to see him where he lived. Upon arriving at his place, he was surprised that I was waiting for him. After a few minutes we got into his car, and we drove somewhere. I remembered asking him, "So how have you been all these years?" He responded, "I just got a new boyfriend, and we have been dating for about a few months now." The moment I heard that I immediately turned away in sadness. I didn't want him to know my heart began to hurt. I thought that we could reconnect, but I guess it wasn't meant to be. I only had one question that I asked the world, and it was, "Why does the heartbreaker get to have a second chance at love when I who have never hurt anyone remains heart broken?" I guess you can say that life is unfair.

During the time we were hanging out, we had talked about certain things. In fact, Eric noticed that I looked more muscular over the years. Over those two years, I worked on myself, and he was attracted to my chest. Whenever I hugged him that day, I smelled him, and it was still that same smell from 2 years ago. It brought back the old memories. He and I became friends for a while, and he apologized for hurting me. After we had separated, he began to message me more. He kept venting to me about how his new boyfriend wasn't giving him enough attention. So whenever he was sad, he would text me constantly. In fact, we would send pictures to each other throughout the day, and it was just like how it was before. Even though he had a boyfriend, I still loved how he gave me so much attention. It was like he cared about me. Dating him again would have been perfect, but a part of me knew it wasn't right. That was because I had a friend named Jeremy who always stole other guy's girlfriends when their relationship wasn't good. He would always flirt with the girl, and it seduced them to the point when they would cheat on their current boyfriends and go to him. I didn't want to do that to Eric or his partner. So one day, I called Eric, and I said to him, "Look, Eric, we need to talk. I thought, and I believe we should stop texting each other." He asked why and I responded, "Because my best friend has ruined a bunch of relationships by flirting with girls who were already in one and I am not going to be that person who would make someone a cheater. I want you to be loyal to him Eric. Relationships are so hard to find at least on my end. I don't want to make you do something you will regret, and for that to happen, I have to stop this." He responded, "Okay I understand and thank you." Then I responded, "Well hey if you two ever break up. Please give me a call." He responded, "No I'm good! You're not right for me due to your personality." That was the end of the story of Eric and me.

Chapter Four

"The First Time I Slept Over"

On the night of March 29th, 2015, I was feeling lonely. I remembered being on the dating app. After swiping through a bunch of profiles. I had gotten matched up with a guy. This guy had brown hair, and he was a mix between Caucasian and Hispanic. After sending him the first message, he responded instantly. He seemed very friendly and very interested in getting to know me. His name was Diego La'Cross, and he lived about 40 minutes from where I lived.

After exchanged messages overnight, we decided to exchange numbers. As soon as I called his phone, he answered and said the first hello. The first thing I thought was "Oh, okay he has a feminine tone. I can be cool with that." We chatted for about an hour and a half, and we just connected on so many levels. He had the sweetest things to say. He told me how adorable I was. After noticing how late it was, we planned to meet up during the week. Once we made the plan, we hung up and went to bed.

I had to wake up the next day at 6 am for school because my class was at 7 am. As soon and I get to school, there was a note on the door that said, "CLASS CANCELLED." Without knowing what to do, I texted Diego and told him about what happened. He hinted that I should come over and I suggested that I wanted to. So I made my way to meet Diego for the first time. I arrived at the house, and I texted him saying that I had just arrived. As soon as he opens the door, I automatically thought he looked way cuter in person. Once I saw him, I gave him a hug.

We walked into his house and went into his bedroom. As we walked towards his room, I looked at him from behind, and I will say, he had a nice ass. Diego was a fashion designer, and he was very creative. The first thing we did was go to his bed and started talking. As the conversation escalated, we eventually just started cuddling. I remember how adorable he was as I held him. He seemed to be very smart which was a big turn on. We kissed for the first time, and it was okay. To be honest, the spark wasn't there, but I was willing to make it work. We agreed that we would date for two weeks and then decide if we wanted to make it official or not. After we had been done spending time together, I had to go back to school for my next class.

The rest of the day we were texting each other romantically. I remember when I called him "Baby" he was so flattered.

Later that day, I was at work, and he asked if I wanted to come over after work, and possibly sleep over if I wanted. OF COURSE, I WANTED TOO. As soon as work was over, I headed to his place. As soon as I got there, he had prepared dinner for me and said, "Yeah if you date me, just know that I might fatten you up with my cooking." I said to myself, "Man, I feel like I am the luckiest guy in the world. Is this really happening?" After I had finished eating, we walked over to his bedroom and took off literally all of our clothes and got under the sheets. It was one of the best night I ever had. Till this day, I will say

that that night was the best memory I had of Diego. I remembered how

we would switch on who held who. During the middle of the night, my

wisdom tooth began to hurt me. He asked what was wrong and I

responded, "It's my wisdom tooth, it's hurting me dreadfully." After

hearing that, Diego began to kiss my cheek multiple times and believe it

or not; the pain went away. I guess they were right when someone says

all you need is a little TLC.

Once the sun rose up, we were looking at each other with big

smiles on our faces. I remember he had a particular smell to him. Not a

bad one just more like as if he showered and he felt a bit too clean. I

remember his dog came up on the bed and Diego said to him, "Hey I

want you to meet someone amazing, this is my boyf...." He paused

himself at that moment, and I just looked into his eyes and smiled.

Before I left, I gave him my Jacket to remember me. He wore that jacket and loved smelling it. He said it smelled like me and judged by the smile on his face; I knew he was going to take good care of it.

Once I drove home we started off pretty good after that, in fact, I remember him telling me that he would sleep in that jacket just so that he could have a piece of me next to him.

Things seemed to be going perfectly until it all went downhill once I got to meet the real Diego. As time went on, he began from texting me every few minutes to a few hours to nothing at all. There had been numerous of times when he would cancel last minute on the plans I've made for us so that he could be with his brothers. Whenever we would go on a date, he would show me attitude. He never appreciated me especially when I paid for most of our meals while we went out. He wasn't the guy I met the first night. Whenever I would try to be happy and be in a good mood, he would always bring it down by being in a grouchy mood. Don't get me wrong there were good times when we would hold hands, but it wasn't enough for me to be happy. We agreed to give it two weeks to decide if we should be official or not. However, because of our conflicts, he maked us wait until a month. I said that I was willing it make it work. There were nights when we would fight, and in the end, he always knew he was wrong. I remember him telling me that he was going to try to change and treat me better, but he never really did. Even though Diego treated me so poorly, I tried my best to treat him with love by texting him good morning and goodnight every day. He would tell me how I was too clingy and it was a turn off to him. I guess his version of dating meant that we didn't have to put too much effort in our relationship. I just wanted to show Diego how much I cared. I don't think I was clingy, but I do believe that he and I just weren't the perfect match.

By dating him, I realized that I felt more alone dating him than when I was single and cuddling with a pillow. Ever since the first night we met, there was hardly ever a time where he tried to make me smile again. I didn't want to let him go until one day I texted him that I was going to get my wisdom tooth out and I texted him that morning, and he replied, "Oh how fun!" I'm sure he was being sarcastic. However, right after I got my tooth pulled out, I waited and waited to see if he would contact me to see if I was okay after getting my tooth pulled out to show that he cared. He never called, and at that moment I knew for sure that he and I were not going to continue.

So I called him, and I asked, "Hey so why didn't you call me to ask if I was okay?" He responded, "Oh? I didn't know I had to." I then took a deep breath, "I thought about it, and I thought about it. And I thought, Diego if you cared then you would have called me. This kind of problem is not what I wanted, I do care about you, but sometimes the little things like this are imperative. It made me realize that I can't just be in a relationship with someone just because I want a relationship. I need someone who will treat me the same way as I will treat them." Diego began to cry as he realized that everything was his fault.

After this breakup, he and I didn't talk for a few months. Over time we got reconnected, and we became friends. He still gives me attitude whenever we hang out, and that is probably something I have to try to be careful. He always told me how he knew that the reason why we didn't work out was because of him. He told me that on Valentine's day of 2016, but we will get to that once we move along with this story. To be honest, I wished I was with him. I always thought that maybe somewhere down the line he and I would reconnect and fall for each other again. Even though we fought so much, I can tell you that Diego was different from John or Eric. Diego was the first guy who liked me and wanted to continue dating me. He didn't walk out that door the next day. Instead, he still wanted to be with me till the very end. Out of all of these guys, I still keep in contact with him.

Chapter Five

"First Time I asked Someone Out in Person"

The fourth guy I dated was the first guy I ever dated where I met him in person. It all happened around June 2015. It was my first ever Gay PRIDE festival. I was invited to go by a friend named Juan Carlos, and he asked me if I wanted to accompany him to the festival. This event was exciting because I didn't even know what it's like at a Pride festival. So I looked it up on images online and saw people with interesting outfits and costumes. So I decided to bring a superhero costume from the 90's. It was a red suit, and the spandex was so tight that the whole shape of my body was exposed. I felt very sexy for the first time. However, when I arrived, I looked around and noticed that I was the only one wearing a costume. Man! I was so embarrassed and uncomfortable. However, a lot of hot guys were coming up to me and asking for a picture. In fact, a bunch of them were asking for my number and grabbing my ass. I guess you can say that the spandex made me the center of attention at the Pride Festival. Anyway back to the story, it was a Saturday afternoon as I walked around the Pride Festival in the sexy costume. As many guys were talking to me, this group that I had spoken to was how I met the fourth guy I dated. There were three guys I was talking to, and I looked at one with short brown hair, and I could tell he was attracted to me just like his friends. So I decided to be spontaneous. I moved closer to him and whispered in his ear, "Out of all your friends, I think you're the cute one." As I stepped back, his face lit up as he couldn't believe what I told him. It was like as if someone out of my league told me I was sexy. He was so speechless that it was so adorable. After whispering in his ear, I quickly said to him and his friends out loud, "Okay, guys happy pride have a good rest of your day." I walked away as that guy I whispered too was shaking in happiness. For the first time, I felt sexy and made someone feel happy. Later that day, we ran into each other again. After we had talked to each other back and forth, he said to me, "I was looking for you. I think you're cute. By the way, my name is Kevin Mitchell". I then replied,

"Yeah I believe that you're cute too. My name is Lorenzo, would you

like to go out on a date sometime?" Kevin smiled. "Yes, I would." As we

stared into each other eyes, we slowly moved closer and closer

together. Kevin and I kissed, and everyone around was watching us.

HOWEVER, The kiss was just terrible. Kevin did not know how to kiss as

all. It felt like a snake moving around. However, I moved passed it and

decided to give him a chance. He was probably one of the worst kissers

I have ever kissed. On the plus side, as I was kissing Kevin, I noticed that

I began to get an erection. Now having an erection and wearing

spandex in public is not a right mix. I then walked away with the helmet

I had on my costume and covered it.

A few days later, it was the time for Kevin, and I to go on our first

real date. I wore my superhero shirt that day, and he wore a gray shirt.

We held hands as we drove to the city of West Hollywood. West

Hollywood is the capital of the LGBT community. It is where everyone is openly gay. I took Kevin there because I have never shown affection

towards anybody before in public. As we walked down the streets, I

held his hand. It felt very nice to be on the other end for once. The

other end was being the guy who had a partner to hold while you're

walking down the street instead of being that single guy who is

watching a gay couple holding hands and wishing that it was you. That

is what made this date very special to me. Kevin was very touchy just

like me. He had no limits, and it was just the right amount of passion.

We walked around the city, and we decided to revisit the spot where

we first met. In fact, we even reenacted how we first met. Later that

day, we decided to eat at this restaurant where we ate unlimited tacos.

He looked so adorable as the light reflected his green eyes. Being with

him in public felt like I finally reached Heaven and I spread my wings for

the first time. Kevin loved holding hands, and despite his terrible

kissing, he was fantastic in different ways. After this date, we began to

continue dating. We went to the movies together, and we agreed to pay only for ourselves. By the way, Kevin loved cuddling, and I was happy to be the big spoon in our relationship.

We sat on the top of the movie theater. Kevin laid down on my lap throughout the whole movie. I remember every once and a while we would kiss each other as my arms wrapped around him. I remember as I held him, he would hold my hand and brush his thumb on the top of my palm. Even though it was a small thing, I remember looking down on him and appreciating the little kinds of affection he would do.

On another date, we went to an abandoned baseball field very late at night. I remember passionately pushing him against the fence and making out with him. One thing about Kevin was that he loved when I would whisper dirty words into his ear. He loved how I whisper to his ear about what I would do to him in bed. He was adorable when he would look at my face. Later that night, we went on the grass and cuddled as we watched the stars. We would always look at each other as we would give pecks of kisses. Now Kevin had to go home at a certain time because he lived in 20 minutes away. Whenever I would say, "Okay Kevin it's time we head back." He would reply to me, "No, a few more minutes? I don't wanna leave yet." Every time he said those words to me, I felt amazing because it felt like he wanted to stay with me during that cold night under the stars. As I would always drive us around, he would always hold my hand while my left hand was at the wheel driving.

Things were going just fine; we would text each other every day and once and a while he would text me good morning. As the weeks went by, I wanted our relationship to keep growing to where we were more emotionally closer to each other. One time I hadn't seen him in a week, so I texted him,"Hey! I miss you!" He responded, "Has it been that long?" Of course, I was expecting something else, but what can you do. As time continued, I noticed that he was more so in touched with his sexual side as oppose to his emotional side. I guess he was in it for more of the passion as oppose to the intimate conversations. Because of this problem, I began to have a hard time connecting with him emotionally. On another date, we went to a restaurant, and we were both silently while we ate. It felt very awkward, and after dinner, we went to a park where we cuddled under a tree. I then asked him, "So where do you see us in the future? Do you see us progressing or anything." He responded, "I have no idea, I mean I like you. I love how we spend our time together." I replied, "Okay, Sorry, it's just for the past few weeks you've been kinda distant." He then responded, "Sorry, I'm just not the clingy type I guess. I'm not the type that needs to be in a relationship. I kind of like being alone."

As more weeks went by, our relationship wasn't growing at all. It felt like the same thing over and over again every time we meet up. It felt more like if we were like friends with benefits than an actual relationship. The passion was right, but it is just that there was no emotional connection. I can tell that he didn't even want to be with me anymore. I had a hunch that he lost interest so I downloaded an old hook up app and I saw that he was online 10 minutes ago. That's when I knew that it wasn't going to workout. In a way, I was sort of happy that he was looking for someone else to hook up with because it meant that I was free. So one day I talked to him, and I told him that I think we should just stay friends. He then said, "Okay! Yeah, I think that would be best." In the end, we ended on good terms, and there was no animosity. Even though this break up wasn't the worst, I've had. Kevin was still important part of my story because he was the first guy I ever asked out in person and went on a date with. He was the first guy I held hands with in public. I guess that was what I liked about him. He was always willing to do anything passionately.

Chapter Six

"First Time I Watched the Sunset"

This next guy I am going to be talking about is a man named Gavin Samuel. The way we met felt like magic. It was so magical that it seemed like fate brought us together. It was the first time I felt like it was destiny. Unlike the other four guys I dated, dating Gavin was the best to date ever. I guess you can say Gavin was the first Prince Charming I ever met. The reason why I say that it felt like destiny was because Gavin wasn't the guy I originally was going to on a date with the day we met.

Before I met Gavin, believe it or not, I was already going on a date with someone else named Cory. In the month of November 2015, I drove out somewhere toward the beach area to meet up with Cory. Cory and I had been chatting for the past week online, and it seemed like we were a good fit. However he lived 40 minutes away, but I was

willing to make it work if we were a match. Upon my arrival, I was

expecting him to be very sexy, charming, and gentlemen like. Little did I

know, once I saw him in person, everything changed. He was a little

average, and I didn't mind at all. I gave him a hug, but he smelled like

he hadn't showered all day. It felt like I was hugging a guy who just got

home from playing football with his friends. He waves his hand at me as

if he was ordering me around to go into his house. Once we were

inside, he rudely forces me to go into his room. The first thing he does

is work on his laptop while I sat on his bed thinking "What the heck is

this guy doing?" He then walked up to me, and we cuddled for a bit and

made out. The moment he kissed me, I felt no spark, and I was so

bummed because this guy didn't impress me at all. As minutes went by,

while he was laying down, I went on my phone and logged onto a

hookup app. Yes! I went on a hookup app while I was on a date, but

keep in mind this was barely even a date. Anywho, the moment I

logged on, I get a message from a very cute guy, "Hello you are very cute." I then replied, "Yeah so are you. Wow, I remember you. We chatted on a dating site about two years ago." He smiled, "Really? :) Wow, I would have remembered a handsome face likes yours if I did." I replied, "Yeah we were chatting, and then you decided to stop responding to me." He was then surprised, "Oh Really? OMG, I am soo sorry, I don't go on that website as much. I hope you can give me another chance. I promise I am a good date." I then said, "Well, believe it or not, I am currently on a date right now." He then said, "Really? Oh sorry! I hope I'm not interrupting anything." I then said, "No, you're fine. The date is going terribly, to be honest." He then replied, "Well if you decide to end it soon, just shoot me a message. Oh, I'm Gavin BTW!" "My Name is Lorenzo! Happy to meet you Gavin, and yeah I'll let you know if I decide to stop this date." Gavin then sends me his phone number, "Yeah man just text me at this number and I'll be waiting."

As a few minutes went by, I began to get a little irritated with my current date. There was just no chemistry. Once Cory walked out of his room to go to the bathroom, I began to put my shoes back on my feet.

As soon as he got back, he then asked, "Where are you going?" I then

replied, "Hey man I'm sorry, but I don't think that it's a match." I felt

very terrible for saying that, but I had to be honest. As soon as I walked

out of the house, I immediately texted Gavin, "Hey I just left his place,

are you still interested in meeting up?" He was surprised, "Wow! Okay

yeah here is my address."

The moment I received his address through the text, I then drove

to his place. Once I parked, I waited for him outside. A few seconds

later, I finally see him walking out. He wore a black T-shirt and some

shorts. He has short brown hair, and he was about 6 feet tall.

"Hi!" I smiled. He then replied, "Hi!" We gave each other a hug,

and as soon as we hugged, his body smelled so good that I took a

moment to smell his shoulder. It was the kind of smell where when you

see a hot guy, and their manly body scent brushed on you as they walk

by. It was also a windy day, and I remembered the wind swept around us as we held each other. As soon as we got into the car, I then asked, "Where shall we go?" Gavin replied, "I don't know if you are down, but maybe we can go to the beach later on today." I then began to share with him about what happened with the guy, and he was so surprised that he tried to make himself look better by telling me things like how he wouldn't do that to me.

The first thing we did was we drove up to a coffee shop to get a little snack. As soon as we bought our drinks, we sat outside on the patio where we began to get to know each other. I remembered putting my leg on Gavin's lap as he began to rub his thumb on it. After exchanging a few more looks, we both moved closer to each other and had our first kiss. At that moment, it was the second time in my life where I began to see fireworks. It was the kind of fireworks I saw with Eric. Gavin's lips were so soft, and he used the right amount of tongue. His facial hair was so smooth that I loved when my face was up against it. I can honestly say that I found magic. The way Gavin kissed was the kissing where you just don't want it ever to stop. The kind where your

heart starts pumping rapidly all you want is for your lips never to

unlock. "Did you just see fireworks?" I asked. "Yes, I did!" His eyes

began to sparkle as each second went by. The way he smiled at me

made him look even more handsome. This whole incident with Cory

and then meeting Gavin felt like destiny. Sure I felt bad for Cory, but

the moment I held Gavin's hand at that coffee table, I knew something

magical had just begun. Gavin smiled, "I love how you like to kiss on the

first date. Most guys I meet aren't like that. It's kinda nice to meet

someone who does." After hearing that, I then kissed him even more,

and I remembered feeling that spark between us igniting as our hearts

began to race.

Later that day, we drove to some house where he was dog sitting.

He was supposed to just take the dog out for a walk. As soon as we

walked out with the dog, we began to walk around the block. I

remember holding his hand while we walked the dog together. I was a little worried about PDA, but I wanted to impress him. Then later that day we went to his place where we cuddled for a bit. We were watching old videos online as we cuddled. I showed old videos of me while I was young and he loved watching them. I remember looking at the reflection of the computer screen. I saw the reflection of our faces. His scruffy face laid on top of my face. He looked so happy, and I just loved the image of how we looked together at the reflection. Was he going to be my first boyfriend? I couldn't believe how happy we looked together. As I paused the world, I remembered thinking, "I can see it now." We were so passionate I loved when his arms were wrapped around me. I remember he told me a story while we were cuddling. He told me about how he one time fell in love with a guy once, and the guy wasn't putting as much effort as Gavin was. They lived very far from each other and Gavin was willing to make it work because he loved him. In the end, Gavin got his heart broken. When Gavin told me that story, I liked him even more for sharing that, and I wanted him to realize that I would never do that to him. We already acted like we were boyfriends as we drove to the beach with his hand on my lap.

Once we parked, he offered to pay for parking. One thing I liked about

Gavin was that he was always willing to pay for me. Even though at

times I would pay, I loved how he would offer. We walked up to the

pier, and I wrapped my arms around him as we watched the waves

come by. I remember giving him kisses on the neck. He loved it so much

that he kept turning his head just to kiss me. Again, I enjoyed the facial

hair. It felt so nice every time I rubbed my face on it. I looked around a

couple of times, and I noticed some people we were staring at us. Some

people just walked off as if they didn't want to be around us. It felt very

uncomfortable holding Gavin in public, but I didn't care because I was

really happy to be with him. I was so glad that not of it even mattered.

It was like no one else existed but him. That was how much he made

me happy on our first date. As the sun began to set on the beach, we

walked on the sand with our hands holding each other. We walked to

the ocean and starting kissing each other as the waves brushed up to

our knees. We loved looking at each other so much. This whole day felt like a fairy tale. Nothing could have been better than this day. How we met and how our day went was so unexpected that I thought about how funny this love story began if we were to tell our friends about it. If we were to become boyfriends down the line, I would be honored to tell how our love story began and how our first date was. You know the stories you hear from older couples who are so in love till this day? The stories where they fell in love for the first time? How magical their sparks felt? Or how the moment they met, they knew they were right for each other? Well, this moment was mine. Gavin was mine that day, and I couldn't have been more honored that he chose to message me on that app. Upon the time when the sun began to set, Gavin and I walked to the sand and dug a little pit for us to sit on to watch the sunset. We sat down side by side and watched the sunset. I looked at him, "Thanks for making me happy today Gavin." He then looked at me and smiled, "Thank you for making me happy Lorenzo." We shared one last kiss as we then watched the sun go all the way down. With our heads together, we watched the sunset till it was finally dark.

By that night, Gavin and I looked at each other one last time and shared a smile. After getting off the beach, we got a little dinner and this time I offered to pay. While we were eating, he opened up to me and said, "Back then, my friends would always bring their partners to movie nights, and I would always feel like the 5th or 7th wheel. Sometimes I wished that I had a boyfriend to hold me during those times." I then got up from my chair and hugged him from the back of his seat and said, "Hopefully when that happens I'll be the one to hold you." He clutched onto my arm so tight that I felt how warm he was. After dinner, I drove him home, and once we parked, we shared one last kiss. The kiss was so passionate that we couldn't stop. It was the kind of kiss where someone you care about is going away for a long time, and you want your last kiss to be memorable. It was love at first sight for me, and just like Gavin, we didn't want to say goodbye. I kissed him one last time and this time I paused my lips onto his lips for 5 seconds until I pushed back, "Goodnight Gavin." Gavin opened the car door, "Goodnight Lorenzo, text me when you get home." I watched

Gavin walk into his house, and once he walked inside, I looked up to the sky and said, "Thank You." I drove home after that and I went to sleep happier than I have ever been.

For the past few days, we were texting each other. Gavin told me he missed me. He said he missed my hugs. We both agreed that in the future we would switch on who would drive to who since we lived about 30 minutes apart. We even decided to take turns on who pays for food whenever we are together. On our second date, we planned to just get some breakfast around his area in the morning. Upon my arrival to his house, he opened his door with just a towel. His eyes glowed with happiness the moment he saw me. It was like as if he had been waiting too long for me. He pulled me inside and started kissing me. "Are you almost ready?" I asked. He replied, "Yeah just let me brush my teeth and put on my clothes. I followed him into the bathroom, and I held him from behind while he was fixing his hair. We both looked into the mirror, and we both agreed how cute we looked together. Later on,

I asked him, "Hey I'm planning on going to this thing with my friends what color do you think looks good on me?" He replied, "I don't know, I can't decide for you." The tone of his voice sounded like as if he didn't care.

As soon as we got into his car, he started talking in a very low tone. It got pretty quiet after a few minutes; I thought he was just feeling a little bit tired. It seemed like something was wrong, but I didn't quite know what it was. As soon as we got to the restaurant, we sat down and looked at the menu. "Wow! all of this looks excellent, what do you think I should try?" I asked Gavin. Gavin then replied is an annoyed tone as if he was lecturing me, "I'm not gonna decide for you. You make your own decisions, OKAY?" I then thought in my mind, "Wow, you don't need to be rude, I am just asking for your opinion." The whole breakfast time was awkward as he barely said a word to me. I looked at him as he just stared down at his food.

After Breakfast, we headed back to his place. I wanted to cuddle with him before I went home. As soon as I laid down on his bed, he grabbed some papers and walked outside. I thought he was just putting them somewhere in the living room. After waiting 10 minutes, I got up from his bed, and as soon as I walk out, he was on the couch studying. Was he trying to push me away? I walked up to him, "Hey I'm just gonna head home." He replied, "Okay bye." We hugged each other, and I left. I had hoped that he would give me a kiss, but it seemed like he didn't want to.

A few days later I called Gavin to ask what was wrong and he said to me, "We need to talk. I think you liked me a little too much and I didn't like how you kept asking for my opinion. I like someone who makes their own decisions, and I like to take things slow. You were moving a bit too fast for me." The first thing I said was, "What are you talking about me moving too quickly. We both moved quickly together. In fact, I thought you and I were on the same level." It felt like my prince charming was just like every other guy I've dated. Someone who just changes their mind the next day without even thinking twice. I guess that perfect love story that had just begun has just become another short story.

I remember how he told me about how he loved someone and that someone broke up with him without even thinking twice. Gavin did the same thing to me. I really cared about him, and I wanted to keep getting to know him, but he turned love away. Till this day, I still want to know if our first date meant something to him. I still remember how Gavin told me that he wished he had a boyfriend to go with him on outings with his friends, and yet he pushed that opportunity away. I guess maybe Gavin didn't look at me as someone he would want to do all that.

Around the time when Gavin broke my heart, the only thing I learned that time was that even the ones who want love the most could break your heart. However, one thing I did learn later on down the road was that I had a big heart full of love and Gavin's heart wasn't compatible to mine. If Gavin is still looking for love till this day, I would tell him this, "Gavin, if someone loves you, think about it before you turn it away because not a lot of people get as many opportunities at finding love as others do. Many people are struggling to find someone. Don't turn away the love that has presented to you. I don't want you to wake up one day and to think what if I had just stayed?" All I know is that maybe I could have been the perfect partner for Gavin, or maybe I was the Mr. Right he was looking for all this time, and he didn't know it. Perhaps, we would have moved in together by now if he had not thrown away an opportunity of finding that I was a good guy that he had been looking for after so long. Now he will never know, and I will never know what would have become. Today in my present, I know there is a guy out there for me. It is someone who will tell me that they are staying and that they are still here to make it work.

Chapter Seven

"The First Time Rebound"

Two months after Gavin, I went through a phase where I had a lot of self-pity. I would constantly tell myself, "No one is gonna love me." I would see gay couples holding hands and feel like the world was mocking me. The past five guys weren't right for me. Why was that? Why did Gavin dump me without even giving me a chance? Am I worth it? Or am I worth being pushed back to the side? Am I worth being loved? So many questions were running through my head, but only one question was at the top, "Why is every guy I date break my heart." I would go on dating sites, and no one would reply back to me. I would go to gay bars, but no one would hit on me or even make eye contact with me. I even tried joining the Queer Alliance Club at my College, but I didn't find any luck there either. I wanted to keep finding love, but a part of me felt like it was pointless because every other guy will just do the same. They will fall for me one day, and tomorrow they will lose interest. At that moment, I wanted to just give up.

This is where Tristan Dagger comes in. It all started one day in February 2016; I was on another hookup app looking for some fun. I was going through the profiles until I found a profile of a white man with red Hair and freckles on his face. Upon looking at his profile, he looked so sexy with his six pack abs and his muscular chest. I then looked more into his profile, and it said something about how he was looking for the one and how he hopes to find him one day. A part of me was like, "Buddy if I was good looking enough and you chose me, I would make you happy every single day till the very end." He seemed nice, but I felt like he was too hot for me. Tristan was like a male model, and I was just simply a Massage therapist with an average built. However, can you blame me? He had a sexy muscle chest and big arms. Without hesitating, I send him a message saying, "Hey man, you will find love one day I promise, and he will treat you very well, and he is gonna make you happy I promise."

"Thanks! That's sweet," he replied. I felt like there is no point in holding back since he might just be like everyone else I dated and then I said, "If I were your type, I would have loved to make you happy every single day. I would do my best to be a good boyfriend." He then laughed, "Haha, Why are you making it sound like I am not interested in you. I think you are really cute." The moment he texted me that, I felt a little bit of joy.

"My name is Tristan, what's your name?" He asked.

"My name is Lorenzo! Happy to meet you, Tristan! Would you be down to go on a date sometime?"

"I would love to!" he replied with a smiling emoji. I'll be honest, Gavin may have been Prince Charming, but Tristan, however, looked like a Knight in Shining Armor. He told me about how he did a lot of films and dancing and asked me to look him up. Once I did, I read his bio that Tristan was a dancer for popular music videos. He can act and sing. He was even friends with some of my favorite singers. I was like wow this guy has a lot of connections in this industry. Tristan will be the first time I ever dated someone who was a Dancer, Singer, and Actor. This male model was the hottest guy I ever went on a date with.

Tristan and I decided to meet at this coffee shop around the area. As I was walking into the shop, he was sitting down waiting for me. He looked exactly like his pictures. Tristan and I gave each other a hug, and we went out for a walk in the park. This red head was about 3 inches shorter than me, and once we arrived at the park, we sat down on a log and began to chat. He looked a bit nervous, and I thought that it was adorable. We talked about movies and male models and all the gossip. He told me about how he dated this one singer who was very conceded. We laughed, and I loved staring into his eyes. As soon as we got into talking about relationships, he began to open up to me. "My boyfriend Abram and I broke up about six weeks ago," said Tristan. "I'm so sorry! You poor thing, are you okay?" I asked. Tristan stared down, "Yeah, he broke up with me and because of him; I lost all my friends. They all ignored me and decided to choose him. It's been a rough six weeks trying to get my life together. I still miss him, to be honest." After hearing that, I just wanted to hug him. Instead, I replied, "I don't know what that's like, but I do know that what happened to you was not very fair." Tristan smiled as we just stared into each other's eyes. I stood up, "Come on, let me take you somewhere that's special to me. " "Where we going?" he asked. "You'll see!" I smiled. My goal was to show him a splendid time. I knew that maybe if I could just get his mind off of his ex-boyfriend, then maybe he could feel better. He was hurt, and at this point, I wanted to try my best to be a friend than a date. However, my sexual attraction to him was so strong that I wished that I could kiss him, but I didn't want to be too pushy.

I took him to the top of a mountain where we were able to see the city lights. We walked to the edge, and I held his hand, but he wasn't gripping my hand. "You don't like holding hands?" I asked. He replied, "I do, but I'm just taking it slow." I then let go of his hand, and we just walked side by side 3 feet apart. I wanted to hold his hand, but I knew that I had to try to respect him since he was still heartbroken. Tristan was like a broken soul, and all of me wished that I could help him feel better. I wanted to be a hero for him and help him heal. There were no words to describing how I felt that moment. I wished that I could tell him that I knew what is it was like to be heartbroken and that if I were to be the one he chose, I would promise to make Tristan happy till the end of my days. I want to be a perfect boyfriend for him. I will always want to make him feel like he has the best partner ever.

While we were walking on the mountain, I just wanted to hold him and tell him that he was not alone. Yes, it may have just been the first date, but I looked at him as a broken soul, and all I want to do is to help him heal. I looked into his eyes, and I could tell he was like me. I could tell he was the type to be very loving and caring. Tristan was the kind to wear his heart on his sleeve. He would put his lover over anyone else. Tristan was loyal, sweet, and a good partner. It just so happens that I am seeing him at the stage where he might have a problem opening up his heart again. I wanted to say to him that I am here. I'm not like the rest. I am different, and I won't break your heart. I would vow to make this relationship work if we were to go past this first date.

Once we arrived at the edge of the mountain, I wrapped my arms around him as we watched the city lights. He didn't seem to enjoy it, and I could feel from his body language. "Are you okay?" I said in a caring voice. "Like I said, I am just taking it slow." I began unwrapped my arms and just let him stand 2 feet away from me as we just enjoyed more interesting conversations about his dancing and about what films he had worked on in the past. He then began to talk about what his ex-boyfriend did to him. I just let him vent since he was the one that was sad. Even though it was not the wisest thing for him to do on the first date, I wanted to be understanding and hopefully a good friend.

Later that night, we went for a little drive to get some Sushi. While on the car ride we blasted the radio and sang some songs together and just had a good time. Later that night, during the drive, he and I were talking more about his music videos that he danced in. I was amazed because he danced with people that I idolized. We arrived at the revolving sushi restaurant and began chatting some more. Being with Tristan was the first time I was on a date with someone where I couldn't have any physical contact. As much as it killed me, I had to keep trying my best not to touch him too much.

After we had finished eating, we agreed to pay for our own meal. As soon as the waitress arrived, I tapped her arm and whispered, "Hey actually, just put it on the same bill, I'll take care of it." Tristan smiled, "You didn't have to do that." I then replied, "No it's okay, I asked you out on this date, and I wanna do right by paying since I'm the one who asked you out." Tristan did something that I could never forget till this day. He looked into my eyes and smiled. It was the kind of smile that I had been waiting for all night. It was the kind of smile where it seemed like he was impressed by how much of a gentleman I was. His smile stood still for a few seconds, "What's wrong?" I asked. His smile grew bigger, "Nothing..." Tristan was finally happy while we sat down at that sushi restaurant and it couldn't have ended any better.

After we had left the sushi restaurant, I took him home. As soon as were in front of his house, I offered to walk him to the door. "You don't have too," he said. "I know, but I want too," I smiled. As soon as were in front of his house, he told me, "Thanks for tonight, I needed it." I looked into his eyes, and I leaned in for a kiss. It was the perfect moment as I slowly moved to kiss him. Suddenly he pushed me away and yells, "HEY NO KISSING!!!" I stood there feeling disappointed. He looked at me and said, "Remember what I said, I wanna take this slow." I replied, "Okay, Tristan have a good rest of your night." I walked to my car feeling very disappointed. I drove home feeling like I wasted my time. The moment I got home, I got a text from him saying, "Hey I'm so sorry about that, I feel awful. It's just I really wanna take this slow; I hope you understand." I texted him back, "I know and it's fine well hey have goodnight I'll talk to you later bye." He replied, "Goodnight." That was the end of our first date.

Two days went by, and I couldn't stop thinking of him. It had been two days since that date, and I hadn't heard from him since. I thought that maybe he just didn't feel like seeing me again. The moment I decided to move on, I get a text from him. "Hey Lorenzo, how have you been?" My heart jumped for joy as soon as I read his text. I was so happy, I walked out of the massage place where I work, and I gave him a call. We talked on the phone, and Tristan was glad to hear my voice and the first thing he said to me made my day, "Hey I had a great time with you Lorenzo, and I kinda wanna to see where this goes." I replied, "Definitely, we can just take it slow and get to know each other a little more. Are you free Friday?" "Yes, I am! What do you have in mind?" I then responded, "How about we go to the beach." "Yes! I haven't been to the beach in so long." "Okay then I'll pick you up 10 am Friday Morning." "Okay, Lorenzo! I'll see you then..."

Once Friday rolled around, We had just arrived at the beach. I wanted to be romantic, so I brought two blankets. One for us to lay on and one for us to wrap around each other. Tristan and I both carried our things as we walked on the sand towards the ocean. We finally picked a spot, and I laid the blanket down. Once we had finally sat down, Tristan starting taking his clothes off until all he wore was a black underwear. It showed his beautiful legs and amazing body. He looked like he would be a sexy lifeguard. Once he had finally sat down, he asked me, "Aren't you gonna take your clothes off?" At that moment, I felt very insecure because I was not as fit as he was. While he wore his tight black underwear, I wore my boxers and a tank top. I felt awkward, but he didn't care about how I looked. He took out his sunscreen and asked me to rub it all over him. Wow, his body felt so good to touch. I wished that we could be passionate because it was at the beach and I pictured us kissing while we watched the waves. However, once we both had put sunscreen on each other, he laid on his stomach and tried to get a tan. Not being able to touch him was very hard for me. I wanted to massage his scalp while he laid down, but he wanted us to take it slow. Once we sat down, I tried to start a conversation with him, "So Tristan, I'm glad you decided to call me for a second date. Did you think I was cool?" He replied, "Yes you were nice." I then asked, "What was your favorite part of our first date?" He responded, "I liked seeing the city lights on the mountains." I then asked, "What do you like about me so far?" Tristan replied in a rude tone, "Quit fishing for compliments." I felt offended by how he responded, so I left him alone by laying on my side of the blanket. I just wanted to know if he liked me or not. I wanted to be sure that he wanted to date me instead of being a distraction from his ex-boyfriend. Feeling sad and alone at the beach while we were tanning, I just laid down on my stomach looking at the sand. I wanted to give him his space while I tried to enjoy the warm breeze. By the corner of my eye, he was staring at me. I refused to want to make eye contact because I didn't want him to see how sad I was.

Next thing you know, I get a kiss on the cheek from him. That kiss on

my cheek was the highlight on the beach. I looked at him and smiled as

I grabbed another blanket and wrapped it around us. We both sat up as

I sat behind him. I wrapped the blanket around us as we watched the

waved come by. That was the very first time I held him. Nothing could

have been better than that as I kissed the back of his neck. That was the

moment when I paused life and tried to make that moment into

memory.

As soon as Tristan and I noticed the sun began to set, we decided

to go for a walk on the pier. So we grabbed our stuff and packed it back

in the car. As we started walking down towards the pier. I let him

borrow my warm jacket so that he wouldn't feel cold. As we were

walking, I remember asking Tristan whether or not he had any idea of

what he was looking for right now. Was he seeking to take it slow with

me so we could build a relationship? I didn't want to date him if we were just going to waste our time. I needed to know because it was my heart on the line. He then said to me, "Lorenzo, I don't need a relationship right now. I mean I like you, but I have to focus on myself. When my boyfriend dumped me, It opened my eyes to something new. I can't be in a relationship if I am screwed up. I have to work on myself first. You're sweet, but I don't want to commit until I am ready. I'm sorry it seems unfair, but since I'm the one who sorta got dumped, I kinda need everything to be on my terms okay?" I remembered thinking, I don't think I can do that. If I date someone, I want to build something and go towards something. I don't want to date someone who is a maybe.

A person who says maybe is someone who is telling the other person that if they disappoint you, at least I gave you the benefit of the doubt, so in the end, it is not their fault since they warned you. I am not looking for a for sure, but I at least want someone who is aiming to get somewhere romantically. The whole night Tristan was very snobby towards me. I couldn't hold him or anything. The whole evening was hurting my heart. However, I just kept putting it in my head that hopefully soon he will come around. No matter how many times he was rude to me that night, I tried my best just to keep hoping that his walls would come down and he would let me hold him. There was a moment when his sunglasses fell, and I went to go pick it up for him until he stopped me and said, "Leave it, let someone else pick it up for me." I stepped aside and thought that it was vulgar.

As the night went on, we went on the edge of the pier where we were near the waves. I kept looking at him and seeing how amazing his eyes looked. I thought in my head that he wasn't a bad guy, he was just hurt and I have to show him that I won't hurt him. He turned to me and said, "Hey I'm gonna go to the bathroom, I'll be right back." As he walked away, I looked to my left, and I see a gay couple holding hands as they were walking past me. The moment they walked away, a tear ran down my eye as I just realized that those two were the perfect example of what I am supposed to feel. Being with Tristan was not

right, and I shouldn't be feeling this way while on a date. I should be

feeling butterflies. I should be feeling happy and passionate. I should be

holding his hand while we share our thoughts, feelings, dreams, and

such. I should be smiling right now instead of feeling lonely. The point is

that I am trying hard to make him happy, but I didn't realize was that

Tristan wasn't even doing the same for me. This position was hard for

me, and the thing is is that it shouldn't have to be this hard. I wished

that I had someone to hold just like how that gay couple was holding

each other. I stared into the ocean. I remembered closing my eyes and

feeling the wind brush through my face as I tried to be strong and not

break down and cry. I opened my eyes, and I saw Tristan walking

towards me to give me a hug. "What was that for?" I asked. He

responded, "You just looked cute there just standing alone." I smiled as

he grabbed my hand while we walked back to my car. Tristan was

finally holding my hand. I was so thrilled because I felt like he was

finally opening up to me.

While driving home from the beach, I had just realized that Valentine's Day was coming up, so I asked Tristan if he had any plans. I was hoping that he would talk about it to see if he would like to go out on a date with me on Valentine's day because I have never had a Valentine before and I would have loved it if he would have been my first. However, he replied, "I don't like Valentine's day, it is too much of a cliche. Originally, I was planning on texting my ex-boyfriend to see if he wanted to meet up on that day. I was going to buy a dozen roses to beg him to take me back. Now I realize that I don't need him. I got to figure out a way to get over him and move on." After hearing that, I held his hand while I could see his eyes watering. I did still care about him but can tell that Tristan still cared for Abram. I wished I was his ex-boyfriend because I want to love him and have him love me too. I wanted to make him happy. No matter how unfair he was treating me or a number of times he was talking about his ex-boyfriend. I was not going to give up on him. In fact, writing this makes me miss him right now. Anywho, we had arrived at his place. We said our goodbyes, and I still had yet to be given a kiss.

A few days later, before Valentine's day, I got a text from an old friend. That friend was Diego, the third guy I dated about a year ago before Kevin and Gavin. I was so happy to hear from Diego because it had been so long. On the day of Valentine's day, we had met up and decided to go to a club together. After we had danced, we went to a park near by, and I began to tell him what had been happening. He responded, "Lorenzo, why are you dating this guy? By now you should have dumped him. Kinda like how when you dumped me." I felt bad that he brought it up, "I'm sorry about that Diego." He held my hand, "No Lorenzo, It was my fault we didn't work out. I admit, sometimes I do wonder what would have been. However, that was the past, and right now you need to make a decision on this guy." "I don't know what to do," I replied in a sad tone. Diego looked into my eyes and said, "Lorenzo, I know you very well, and you know in your heart that you would make a great boyfriend. I also know you very well to the point that I know what your decision will be with this guy." "Thank you, Diego," I smiled. Diego and I gave each other a kiss as we spent the night hanging out and walking around holding hands.

Two days later, Tristan and I went on another date at a ranch. We walked around looking at the horses, and the connection was not there. He kept making it clear that everything we did romantically was on his terms. I couldn't hold his hand unless he allowed it. I couldn't wrap my arms around him unless he let me. Finally, he made it clear to me that only he could put his hands around me. As we finally got into the car, he started putting his hands all over me trying to be very sexual. "What are you doing?" I asked. He replied, "Just relax, let's just have a little fun." While it came time for a kiss, he slowly had his lips one inch away from me. I stood still feeling afraid of what was happening. We both paused as I was waiting for him to kiss me. I remember thinking in my head, "Please kiss me, Tristan. Please!" After waiting for a few more seconds, Tristan pulled away and said, "No, you don't get a kiss just yet." At that moment, I then realized that I wasn't happy and I will never be happy. This guy is going to ruin me just like how Diego did emotionally. However, this guy was way worse and far worse than Diego.

The date had finally ended, and I've had enough of Tristan's behavior towards me. So I gave him a phone call, "Hey we need to talk." He replied, "About?" I then began to vent out the emotions that I have kept since day one. I called him out on his attitude and how his behavior was unacceptable. I said to him that just because his boyfriend broke his heart, it is not an excuse to behave so rudely all the time. After that phone call, Tristan hung up the phone, and I thought that it was the last time we had ever heard from each other.

The next morning, I felt sorry for what I said to Tristan, so I tried calling him a few times, but never got an answer. I remember Tristan telling me how he use to be a hopeless romantic and how much he gave to his boyfriend in the past and how he never received it back, so instead, he decided to harden his heart, and I was the first victim of that hardened heart. A part of me still cared about Tristan. I cared about him so much, I had to put away my pride, and do something that I would never do.

A week later, I stopped by Tristan's place. I knocked on the door, and when he opened it, I asked him if we could talk outside. He walked outside and said, "You think you have the right just to come here uninvited? That's the problem with you Lorenzo you don't listen. You're too stubborn, and that's why you and I will never work out." I looked at Tristan in the eye and said, "Look, I didn't come here to get you back. That's because I know we aren't right for each other, and I'm sure you know that too." He replied back, "You don't know that Lorenzo because you're so impatient." I raised my voice, "Tristan, I didn't come here to argue with you!" Tristan's eyes widened as he knew I was serious. I looked at Tristan straight in the eye and said, "I came here as an adult to say I was sorry about what I said, that's all. I am not here to ask you out again. I am here because I own up for what I said. Which is something I'm sure you can't relate too, right? If you question why it is because I believe you're something special to me." Tristan's eye began to tear up, "Okay Lorenzo, I'm listening." I continued with my little speech, "When you told me about how you were once a hopeless romantic, it made me like you even more. Then when you said about how your boyfriend broke your heart, it made me like you to where I would do anything to make you happy. Oh my God Tristan, can't you understand?" Tristan's eyes began to water as I began to explain, "Tristan, two months ago I got my heart broken too. Even though he and I only dated for three weeks, I still was able to relate to you. I know how it feels to care about someone and then wake up to them not feeling the same way anymore. You and I both got our hearts broken. I wanted to give you the love you have always wanted. I thought that maybe you and I could give each other that special piece in our hearts.

That piece you and I have been searching for so long." My voice slowly calmed down, "I guess sometimes life isn't very fair because we met at a wrong time. I do want to be with you, Tristan. I don't wanna be your enemy, I want to try this again if you are still interested." Tristan wiped his tears, "Wow this was intense. I had no idea this was how you felt." I slightly smiled, "I guess that's what happens when you bottle things up." Tristan replied, "Look, I'll think about it. Thanks for coming here. I'll call you when I have made my decision."

As another week went by, Tristan had called me and said, "Hey I thought about it long and hard, and I've decided that I don't want to try this again. There was a spark, but it wasn't developed enough. Because of how you yelled at me that one night, I realized that I couldn't be with someone like you." The last words I said to him were, "Look I saw your flaws, and I accept them, if you can't accept my flaws now that you've seen them, then it's true we probably aren't the perfect match." Tristan took a deep breath, "Goodbye Lorenzo." Tristan hung up the phone, and that was the last time Tristan, and I ever heard of each other. I don't believe that Tristan was wrong for me. In fact, I think that he was right for me. It is just that life brought us together at a wrong time in life.

As week later after my last encounter with Tristan, I went on a hookup app, and I get a message from this one cute guy. I looked at his face, and it took me a few moments before I realized that it was Tristan's ex-boyfriend. I know! What are the odds? He messaged me saying, "You are cute! I'm Abram by the way." I then replied, "Hi Abram, I'm Lorenzo, what are you looking for on here?" As I messaged him, I was so mad because I felt like it was because of him that Tristan treated me so terribly. Abram replied, "Just fun for now; I just got out of a relationship a few months ago." I sarcastically replied back, "Gee, I wonder what happened. Who dumped who?" Even though I knew what happened, Abram replied, "I broke up with him, he and I weren't right for each other. I still care about him, but he needed to find himself, and

I was just in the way." I thought to myself; this Abram guy seems like a nice guy. "Was he a red head?" I asked. He replied, "Yeah? How did you know?" I then responded, "Was he also a dancer?" Abram got a little freaked out, "Wait! Do you know Tristan?" I then replied back, "Yeah, I dated him and he just dumped me last week." Abram felt surprised, "I'm so sorry Lorenzo. Wow! What are the odds of us two meeting huh?" I responded, "Yeah, well I cared about him, I wished he and I had more time to get to know each other. It seemed like he would have been a good partner for me if he had given me a proper chance." Abram felt sympathetic, "Wow, it looks like you loved him." I then replied, "Maybe I did, I don't know." Abram then suggested, "Want to come over? Maybe we can talk about it." I replied, "Sure what's your address?"

Later that night, I had arrived at his place. I walked in through the gate, and he stood there waiting for me. We looked at each other, and we gave each other a hug. "Wow, you're even cuter in person," Abram smiled, "Would you like to come inside?" I slightly smiled, "Sure."

We entered his bedroom, and we laid on his bed talking. "So tell me what happened?" he asked. I then replied, "I'm okay right now, it's still a little fresh to me." "Well let me tell you this, Tristan is not what you think he is." "What do you mean?" I asked. Abram replied, "When we dated, we always fought, he always had me pay for our food. He always slept over every night to the point when my roommates would get mad because he was staying over and he wasn't even paying rent. It was just an unhealthy relationship, and he needed to work on himself. I still love him, but I ended it because I want him to be able to take care of himself." I smiled, "I'll be honest before coming here, I was thinking about punching you in the face." Abram laughed, "Well I'm glad you didn't." Here I am sitting in a room next to Tristan's ex-boyfriend. What happened next made the whole night enjoyable. Abram put his hand on my face, "Lorenzo, you are a good man. Trust me, I can see it. You deserve love; I hope you know that. You are gonna make a great

boyfriend to someone one day." "You think so?" I asked. Abram smiled,

"Of course I do, dude you're freakin HOT!!!" As Abram and I looked at

each other's eyes, our lips moved closer together. Time stood still as we

had our first kiss. As that moment, we looked at each other as we

began to take out clothes off. It was the kind of passionate kiss where

you are crazy for each other to the point where you rip each other's

clothes off. "Let's not tell Tristan about this okay?" Abram quickly

asked. "Oh, most definitely not!" We went under the sheets and began

to make passionate love.

By the time it was one in the morning, I had started getting

dressed to go home. "Remember Lorenzo," said Abram while still under

the sheets, "Just hang in there, and you will find what you're looking

for." I looked at him, "Well, for now, I don't know if I should even keep

looking. Thanks for tonight Abram." Abram smiled, "Anytime buddy, I'll

see you around." That was the first and last time I ever saw Abram. Yes,

I did hook up with Tristan's ex-boyfriend. It was a rebound triangle from where I was standing. Will I Lorenzo find what I am looking for? I don't know! All I do know was that someday I would be okay. Thank you, Abram, for helping my to feel better. If it weren't for Abram, I wouldn't have moved on from this.

If there is something I learned from dating Tristan it is that I will never become like Tristan. No matter how many times a guy like Tristan, Gavin, or Eric breaks my heart, I will never change the parts of me that will make myself a good partner. I will never harden my heart because if I do meet the right guy, he will see how much of an amazing person I have become. That is something I promised myself till this day.

Chapter Eight

"The First Time I Heard I Love You"

As the year passed, I had already given up on love. Something was wrong with me. John, Eric, Diego, Kevin, Gavin, and now Tristan. Why is it that I cannot stay with a guy. Maybe I was too pushy, or maybe I was opening up to them too soon, or maybe I wasn't mature enough. All I knew for sure at that time was that every guy I met was just the same. Finding a man to love me for me is a challenge. I see couples together, and I hate looking at them. It mocks me every time I see them being happy. Why can't I have that? I don't know. I see young men my age walking down the streets holding their partner's hand, and it bothered me every time. It felt like life was punishing me with the curse of always finding Mr. Wrong. I was already 23 years old, and I always see videos of teenage gay couples kissing, and I feel sad because they found love early in life. I see videos online that are titled the boyfriend tag as they show how happy they are. I knew I wasn't going to die alone. However, I kept asking myself how many more years must I go feeling lonely. It's like every guy who is boyfriend material is already taken, or the ones who are single and boyfriend material are not interested in me. What's the point? The next guy I'll meet will probably do the same. Just like John, Eric, and Gavin. I will now tell you the last story about the seventh and final guy of my story. This story will become more heartfelt because he was the first guy to say to me, "I love you." This last story is about a man named Joe Falls.

It all started after 10 pm Thursday night in October 2016. My co-worker Taress and I had just got off work from the massage spa, and I offered to take her home. "Thanks love for the ride," she said. "Have a good night Taress," I responded. The moment she entered her apartment, I took out my phone and logged onto a hookup app. The same app where I met Gavin. While I was online, I get a message from someone who was very cute. He has short red hair just like Tristan. His bio said he was 5 feet and 7 inches tall. "Hey Cutie!" He messaged. "Hey Handsome, How are you?" I replied.

"Feeling good, I had a long day today."

"Oh? What are you looking for on here?" I asked. He replied, "Kinda looking for a cuddle buddy tonight. I kinda want someone to hold me." This guy was so charming, and sexy. His profile picture was of him at the beach. After exchanging a few more messages, I finally headed over to his apartment.

I had finally arrived, and I see Joe waiting for me outside. He wore a tight muscle shirt and some shorts. His body was so sexy as I watched him open my door and sat in the passenger's seat. He had green eyes and some facial hair. "I'm Joe Falls by the way." "My names Lorenzo!" The both of us couldn't stop staring at each other as we entered his parking garage. I immediately grabbed his hand as I was driving. The attraction was so strong that once we parked, we gave each other a kiss. "Let's go inside?" he asked. Once we walked out of the car, we began to go to the elevator. I couldn't stop staring at him. His body was so beautiful, his legs were so thick, and he had a bubble butt.

We finally entered his apartment and as soon as we got into his bedroom. I pushed him onto the bed, and I start kissing him passionately. His hands touched my body all over as my hands were holding the back of his head. I grabbed his hands as I pinned him down and kissed on his neck. He moaned quietly as my tongue slowly moved up to his ear. As I stared into Joe's face, his eyes glow with such a spark. It was as if he was falling in love with me. It was the kind of spark that was much stronger than any guy I have ever dated. "Joe, you're so handsome." "So are you Lorenzo." The two of us began taking each other's clothes off. His naked body felt so amazing as we both pressed against each other. Holding Joe felt different. I have cuddled with many guys, but for a moment I felt like I was home. It was like we were two halves of a heart that had finally connected. As hours went by, our passion grew stronger as we kept kissing under the sheets. "Oh,

Lorenzo!" He whispered. His voice was so masculine and so soothing. I loved every single word he said especially when he said my name.

In my mind, I knew that maybe this is just like the other guys. I will like him, and then he might not feel the same the next day. Feeling as if I had nothing at all to lose, I took advantage and treated Joe as if he was mine. "Joe," I murmured. "You're mine," I smiled. "I'm yours baby..." He breathed softly. I remember rubbing his back while he laid on my chest. I kissed his forehead multiple times as he rubbed his face onto my chest. I told him, "If I were your boyfriend, I would hold you like this every night." He was smiling as he couldn't believe the words that were coming out of my mouth. "I would have to be your boyfriend one day baby!" He smiled. I looked at him, "Yeah and wake up to your beautiful face every day, and then take our dog to the park. You and I are cuddling on a Sunday Morning." Joe replied softly, "Yes Baby! I love that. Please tell me more." I then continued, "I'll hold your hand whenever we are in the movie theater's, watch the sunset while we lay on the sand of the beach, look into your eyes, and realize that this is the man I am gonna be with for the rest of my life. Just you and me against this world." Joe replied, "Wow, where have you been my whole life? Lorenzo, you are something else." As Joe kept loving every single word that was coming from my mouth, he then said something that changed everything, "Oh Lorenzo! I love you!" My eyes opened wide as I heard him say that. It was the first time someone ever said I love you.

Even though I knew it wasn't love, to me it was the first time anyone has ever said that to me. No matter if it was just puppy love or not. I cherish those three words till this very day. Till this day, I still don't know what love is, but when Joe said that to me, I somewhat had the idea. It was a magical night, and we were talking about love and what we would do together if we were together. Joe was moving a little bit too fast for me, but I didn't care because the guys I was with in the past dumped me for moving too quickly. I didn't want to be like them, so I at that point decided that I will make this work because Joe is just like me. The conversation happened almost all night as we cuddled. Of course, I was the big spoon. I remember the whole night we were tossing and turning. It kept us up half the night because we couldn't stay still for too long. My most significant position was when I held him from behind with my face behind his head as my breath brushed down his neck, and as my arms were wrapped around him, our hands locking onto each other's hands. Our feet would rub together as the whole night continued. As he laid on my chest, I looked up at the ceiling, and I once again paused at this moment. I made sure time stood still at this moment as this handsome guy was laying on my chest with his hand holding my hand. I thanked God for this time, and I don't know if I was ready to give dating another try, but at this moment, I was feeling something loving and hopeful.

As soon as the sun raised up, I woke up with Joe laying on my chest. He opens his eyes, looks up, and smiles, "Good Morning baby." I smiled back, "Good Morning Babe. Last night was fantastic wasn't it?"

"It sure was," He smiled as he began to kiss my chest. Waking up to him felt like I was home. "So what are you up to today?" I asked. "I have to go to work later at 10, how about you?" He asked. "I'm gonna go to an aquarium with my friend Sam. Joe, if you have time, would you want to go maybe get some breakfast?" He then smiled at me, "Sounds good to me Baby!"

Once we got into the car, Joe and I immediately held hands as we drove to the nearest restaurant for breakfast. I remember asking Joe if he had a car and Joe opened up to me about how he got into a car accident when he was very young, and it traumatized him. I then said to him, "Well hey if you and I work out, I'll be doing the most driving." Joe then smiled at me, "What do you mean if? I think we'll be good." His confidence about us was a big turn on. Even though we had just met last night, I could tell he was opening up his feelings as I felt his thumb brush onto my hand as we were holding hands.

As soon as Joe and I arrived at the restaurant, we had finally sat down at a booth. Once we sat down, we just began talking about each other. Getting to know him was very amazing. He had a dream to become a bartender. I remember telling him how I wanted to travel and visit places. How I wanted to go ice skating or horseback riding. He told me about how he wanted to travel around the world. I then started showing him pictures of me of when I was young, and he thought I looked very cute. As the amazing conversations continued, I remember Joe held my hand as we were eating our food. I was still very hesitant to even go through with seeing if I wanted to date again. Suddenly as I looked to my right, I see a gay couple eating breakfast with their son sitting with them. I looked at them and smiled as they seemed to be a very happy family. As I looked at Joe, he appears to be a charming and genuine guy. I didn't know how to feel, but I sure felt happy that I got to meet him. As soon as we got our bill, we both agreed to split the bill. As I drove him to work, he said to me, "I can't wait to see you soon

Lorenzo. Thanks for having breakfast with me." I smiled as I drove, "I feel the same way."

"I love you," He smiled as he stared into my eyes. "I love you too," I replied with a happy, but sad expression. It felt like this reality wasn't real. Did this guy like me? Is life going to do this to me again? All I could think about was that I have to see and hope that my heart will be okay with whatever happens. Once we parked by his workplace, we gave each other a kiss. He couldn't stop staring at me as he walked out of the car. I watched him walk away as he entered the building where he worked.

As the days went by, Joe and I kept texting and calling each other. He was pretty good with communicating with me. He was so sweet, but I was still hesitant to open up. Until one day, he told me over the phone, "Lorenzo I care about you, and I do hope you know how much I care." The tone of his voice was so genuine and so loving, I had finally believed him. At that moment, I said to myself, let's try this one more time.

Later during the week on a Saturday night, we decided to meet up to get dinner. I had just picked Joe up from his apartment. As we were driving down the freeway, I noticed we were driving into the sunset. We both laughed as we saw it. "Looks like an ending to a movie where we drive towards the sunset huh?" I asked. "Yeah, it sure does!" Joe smiled. We had finally gotten to my hometown where I wanted to show him where I grew up. He was very intrigued by the things he saw. I then took him to the mall where we walked around for a bit. We went to a cookie shop where I bought us a giant cookie. It has a lot of frosting on it, and the first thing I did was break a piece off and fed it to him. As soon as he ate the piece, he immediately cut another piece of the cookie, and he fed it to me. It was so sweet how we did that for each other. Seeing the loving smile on his face made me feel complete. However, that cookie was just the beginning of that night.

Later that evening, we walked around my city trying to find a restaurant for us to eat at, but every place was full. The whole time we were searching, we would give each other kisses and take pictures of each other. People looked at us, and they could tell how happy we both were together. I love how Joe would regularly grab my hand while we were walking. I loved every time we stopped to look at each other in the eyes until it leads up to a kiss.

We had finally reached a Chinese restaurant that wasn't too busy. We went inside and sat down at a booth. We sat across from each other. The whole time during dinner our hands would grab each other. Joe and I were physically inseparable. We both love feeling each other's touch. We both ordered Orange Chicken, Beef Broccoli, and some fried rice. So much laughter and enjoyment towards each other. There was not a moment on that dinner table where my smile went away. Joe had finally opened up my heart, and I was ready to give dating a chance again. While eating, I had put my leg under the table and rested it on the seat where Joe was sitting. He looked to his left and saw my foot. The moment Joe saw it, he began to rub my ankle. That touch took my breath away as he kept his hand there for quite a bit.

As soon as dinner was over, Joe and I went out for a walk. I was carrying the leftover food we planned to take home. As I carried it, he grabbed it from me and said, "Baby, no I'll hold it. You've driven us here, let me do the work." Joe was so sweet, and it gave me butterflies to see how much of a gentleman he was. He was something special, but the next part of the date is where things turned interesting.

I took him to my old high school where he was fascinated by the structure. We walked around as I showed him every single spot I hung out at during the four years I had been there. Joe and I went up to the third floor where we watched the view of the school and felt the wind brush through our faces. He held me from behind as I could feel his arms tighten as he held me. I turned around and pressed my face against his face. That's the moment when I said to myself, this man will become my partner one day.

The whole time we walked around, our hands with locked together and imagined us in high school together as a couple. I never got to hold someone's hand in school before. I guess this moment kind of makes up for it even though no one was around.

I then took him to the football field where I had a confession to make. "Joe, I have something to tell you." "What is it, baby?" He asked. "I never had a boyfriend." "Really? Why not? After getting to know you the past few days, it seemed like you would have had." I then told him about the six guys I dated and how it all ended the same, "Well it all started when I was about 18 years old when I met John............"

As we stood still by the stairs, I told him my story and the tears from his eyes were so genuine. I could tell he was listening. By the time I finished my story with Tristan, Joe had held me so tightly and said,

"Lorenzo, you are an amazing person, and I appreciate you opening up to me about this. I love you!!"

"I love you too," I replied. Joe and I held each other for a few more minutes as he felt so sorry for what my heart went through. At that moment, we both agreed that we would try to be in each other's lives and to someday become boyfriend somewhere down the line as we got to know each other a little more. I felt so confident in Joe; I felt sure that he wasn't like the other guys. He then looked at me and said, "Baby, let's go home." Joe made it seem like his apartment was my home too. The moment he said that I first thing I said to myself was, "Joe, you are my home."

As we had arrived at his place, we walked around shirtless and stared at each other through the mirror in the bathroom while we were brushing our teeth. It did felt like we were living together.

We had finally gone to bed, and it was the perfect ending to this date as we held each other throughout the night. We love each second that passed by, as we kissed so passionately. It was the kind of passion I had never felt with anyone before. I remember Joe kissing every inch of my chest to the point where he left about three hickeys. Half the night we just talked and laughed. We touched each other faces as we kept gazing into each other eyes with our feet gently rubbing together, and our hands locked. Later on, during our conversations, Joe would lay on my chest leaving me to kiss his forehead continuously.

Sometime during the night as we were changing positions, I held him from behind, and I whispered in Joe's ear, "I love you." Joe was half asleep and replied in a low voice, "I love you too." The reason why I liked when he said I love you was because it felt so real. I don't know if the meaning behind it was right, but all I knew was that my heart finally knew how it felts to hear it. Holding Joe while sleeping felt amazing, even though we tossed and turned. I remembered thinking that this man was mine. I stared at the back of his head while he was deeply asleep and said, "Thank you, Joe, for opening up my heart." Even though Joe was asleep, I meant every word I said while I whispered in his ear hoping that maybe he could hear it in his dreams.

The next morning, we both woke up with our faces parallel to each other. "Good morning Baby," Joe smiled. "Good Morning Joe," I replied. We both then cooked breakfast together and ate at his bedroom. After exchanging laughs and kisses, he walked me to my car. After giving a kiss goodbye, I finally drove off. I drove home feeling triumphal and confident that my life was going to change. I felt like Joe might have broken the pattern that I have been trying to break for the last five years.

However, what happened next is what made me think, I knew it was too good to be true.

I waited for him to text me all day, but I never got one. Two days later I finally called him, and he finally answers. "Hey, you! What's up?" he answered. "Hey is everything okay? I haven't heard from you in the last two days."

"Sorry buddy, I've been busy here at work. We're working on some new projects. It's going to be crucial, so I will need to be 100 percent focused on it." My heart began to drop, "Are you saying you won't have time for us?" Joe took a deep breath, "I'm sorry Lorenzo, I guess I realized that my job is more important. It's who I am, and it's what I love to do. I'm sorry, I guess I'm just good at screwing things up when it comes to relationships." I held back my emotions, "No Joe, don't feel bad I don't have any regrets, if I never met you, I never would have understood what it felt like to be loved so much. It's because of you I got to see the parts of me that had never been brought out. Joe follow your dreams and maybe somewhere down the line we will cross paths again." Joe then laughed, "Yeah maybe." I closed my eyes, "Goodbye Joe." Without even replying, Joe hung up the phone leaving me alone once again.

The best part about Joe was that he brought out the best in me. Just like how Eric and Gavin brought out the best in me. The best of me is that I'm loving, caring, passionate, and affectionate. I'm glad Joe, and

I met, and that part of history remains in my heart.

Chapter Nine

"Who I am Today"

This last chapter is about who I became today. Five years have gone by, and I have had seven attempts with seven different guys, and it all ended the same. People tell me the same things every day. They always tell me to be patient. Stop looking for love and love will find you. If you keep looking for it, you won't find it. Love yourself before someone can love you. Lastly my favorite, just have fun, you're too young to settle down."

My worst fear isn't that I won't find love. No, my worst fear is finding love so late in life. I am in my early 20's, and I want to have the opportunity do things with someone romantically. I want to understand what it feels like to hold someone's hand while I am walking down the street. I want to know what it's like when I wake up every morning with someone's arm wrapped around me. I want to know how it feels when you are driving home late at night with your partner asleep in the passenger's seat. I want to know what it feels like to cuddle with someone on the couch while watching a movie on an expensive big screen TV that we both saved up to buy together. I want to know what it feels like to go to the park and play with a puppy we both got together. I want to know what it's like to fight with someone and not have to worry about if they will leave me so quickly. I want someone who will show me the world that I have yet to discover. I want to know what I feel like to just have that kind of a best friend. I can live without a partner. I just choose not to.

My mom once told me that gays are not meant to find love because all they do is want sex and they cheat on each other. FOR ME, I want to prove them wrong. I want to become a good partner. I want to be someone who will always love their partner, to show affection, and to appreciate him for being in my life.

One thing I learned from all these men is never to let what happened to destroy the elements that make me a perfect partner. If you are a MR. RIGHT, don't let MR. WRONG turn you into a MR. WRONG as well. We can mature and change our approach, but never change the characteristics we have that make us a perfect partner. Another important lesson is that no one was the bad guy here. The whole point of dating is to find the person you're most compatible. I don't blame Joe or any of the other guys for not wanting to be with me because it's just that we weren't a match. It just so happens that they were the ones to see it first. Just like how I saw it first with Diego, Kevin, and Tristan. My only hope for all of them is that they will find their soulmate as well or at least find what they are looking for.

For those men out there who are also hopeless romantics, just know that we are all here looking for the same thing and that is to meet people as friends or find that special someone, so please let's all respect each other and understand that we are on here for the same reason.

To all of you reading this, always remember if you are feeling lonely, it means that your heart is supposed to be filled and I promise you it will happen. Maybe not today or tomorrow or even next year, but someday it will come. Love does exist, but the only sad truth is that some people get it earlier in life than others. However, the only thing we can do is have patience. That is something I am still trying to have. I'm trying to be patient to wait my turn to find love one day. When I do meet that right guy, I promise to make him feel loved. Encourage him to follow his dreams with me by his side. Spend every Christmas together and hopefully have a room full of children with our dear friends spending the holiday with us.

Maybe that is why life makes us wait for so long. Maybe life wants to turn us into Prince Charmings so that when we do find our soulmate, we will treat them very special because the wait has been so long.

Maybe life wants us to appreciate them once we find them because not everyone can get a partner or boyfriend so easily. Maybe it is to give us that idea that love is so special that we should never take it for granted once it's given.

Before, I use to hate seeing couples holding hands. I use to envy them because they had what I have always wanted. I use to always ask myself, "How did they do it? Was it by luck that they found each other? Did the God's favor them so much that they decided to match them up? Is life trying to make me suffer? Or is life trying to make me the man I am supposed to be before I meet him? The only question I have today is, "When will I be okay?"

There are many people like me out there who are feeling lonely. No matter how many times I've been denied, love. I wouldn't wish that on anyone. No matter who we are, everyone deserves love. Nowadays, when I see a couple holding hands, I applaud them because they made it this far. They made it farther than I have yet to have gone. My wish is to ensure that everyone finds true love one day. If I could, I would take the honor of being Cupid and help everyone find their soulmate. However, that's how I use to think. Now I know that cannot happen because those of us who are single, each of us have a destiny that we must accomplish before we meet the one. I know that life is trying to turn me into the man I am supposed to be. I wish I could help everyone find love. I know that I can't do that, but I do know that I can help one person. Hopefully, there will be much more who will find their happy ending.

There is one thing that I have figured out in life. It is that a boyfriend isn't just a title someone is given when they like each other. To me, a boyfriend is someone who makes it work when you two have a fight. Someone who is willing to be emotionally and spiritually available. Someone who will put your needs before themselves. Someone who sees and loves you for who you are good or bad. Someone who is not afraid to tell you when you are wrong. Someone who knows how to put a smile on your face when you are down. Most of all for my sake I guess, someone who can't wait to see you again once they walk out that door. I guess in my way; I already am a boyfriend. I just don't have a partner.

One stormy night, I was driving in the rain clearing my thoughts. That's when I thought about writing this book. As I was driving, I remembered looking at the passenger's seat next to me and tried to picture Joe sitting right there holding my hand while I was driving. I miss being touched, and I miss the feeling of having someone like me back. Throughout all of these guys, I don't have any regrets of dating them. I thank God every day for allowing me to feel loved even though it was for a short period. As I was with each of these guys I remembered pausing time for each one of them. As I held them, I would close my eyes and understand what I was feeling. It was the feeling of being completely happy. It was that feeling of being happy that I made sure I would always remember. As I finally got home I wrote down a letter to my first boyfriend and here is what it said:

Dear Future 1st Boyfriend:

By the time you read this letter, we will already be in a relationship, and I hope it has been at least a few months into our relationship for you to read this. Right now 12/22/16 12:38 AM I am writing this to you now because I want you to meet the guy I was before I met you. In my days now, I thought about you every night. Imagine you holding me while I'm sleeping. Even though I don't know what you look like yet, I am so glad we will be together one day. I hope I find you soon Babe!!! You're my first. I just want to say thanks for letting me be your boyfriend......

The rest of the letter is for him to read when I find him. I always wonder how other people can live with being lonely. I am only 23, and I wonder how other people much older deal with it. Throughout all of this, I learned one important thing.

"Life is never fair, and I know being lonely is never easy, but falling in love is not the only way to live."

I found peace with where I am today. Yes, I still have lonely nights, but I also figured out a way to be happy. I have a job, a loving family, and friends. I have goals and dreams. I am healthy and well. Most of all, so much good has happened to me over the years while being single. Sure I would have loved to have a partner during those times, but at least I have memories of my life that will last a lifetime. I want to find my soulmate. I am in a world where I have what I need. I would like him to be a part of that world.

One night when I went to bed, I had a pillow right behind my back, and I imagined it was someone behind holding me. As I looked into the stars, I began to close my eyes. Suddenly I woke up in a room. It was a wooden room with bright lights coming down from the windows. "Where am I?", I asked.

"I knew you'd be here," a familiar voice said to me. I turned my head, and I saw my future self standing in front of me. "You're me?!" I said in shock. He smiled, "Yes I am, and I have been waiting for you buddy." I asked him, "Why am I here? How did I get here?" I then looked at his outfit, and he was wearing a white tuxedo. It was so soft, and it was almost as white as snow. I asked, "Whats the occasion today?" He smiled, "Well Lorenzo, What do you think?" I looked at his ring finger, and I notice a wedding ring. "You're married?" I asked. He smiled, "Well yeah the wedding party is outside, and I should be getting back before our husband wonders where I am."

I had so many questions I wanted to ask him. I asked him, "What's his name?" He responded, "You know I can't tell you that." I then looked down in despair. My future self walked up to me and said, "What I can say is that he is everything you've ever wanted and everything you've ever hoped for. He is going to love you so much, Lorenzo. Believe me; he is worth the wait. Lorenzo let me tell you something that you will learn soon, and it is that your soulmate already loves you and he is coming as fast as he can to find you. Everyone deserves true love, do not let all those heartbreaks take that hope away from you because it is that love and hope in your heart that makes you Mr. Right" I then began to cry happily, "Really? What makes our husband different from the rest?." My future self then walks up towards me and slowly says, "You'll know it's him when he tells you......... Let's make this work!"

"Let's make this work?" I repeated, and I was trying to process this information into my head. Suddenly I hear the door open and a happy voice saying, "Where is my newly wedded husband?"

Before I could see who it was, the room began to turn blurry. I tried blinking a couple of times, but by the time I opened my eyes one last time, I was back in my room. I had then realized that I had woken up from my dream, but then I looked out the window and wondered. "Was that a dream?"